THERIZINOSAURUS

and Other Dinosaurs of Asia

by Dougal Dixon

illustrated by
Steve Weston and James Field

PICTURE WINDOW BOOKS
Minneapolis, Minnesota

Picture Window Books
5115 Excelsior Boulevard
Suite 232
Minneapolis, MN 55416
877-845-8392
www.picturewindowbooks.com

Printed in the United States of America.

Library of Congress Cataloging-in-Publication Data
Dixon, Dougal.
Therizinosaurus and other dinosaurs of Asia / by
Dougal Dixon ; illustrated by Steve Weston &
James Field.
p. cm. — (Dinosaur find)
Includes bibliographical references and index.
ISBN-13: 978-1-4048-2261-0 (library binding)
ISBN-10: 1-4048-2261-5 (library binding)
ISBN-13: 978-1-4048-2267-2 (paperback)
ISBN-10: 1-4048-2267-4 (paperback)
1. Dinosaurs–Asia–Juvenile literature. I. Weston, Steve,
ill. II. Field, James, 1959- ill. III. Title.
QE861.5.D665 2007
567.9095–dc22   2006028003

Acknowledgments
This book was produced for Picture Window Books by
Bender Richardson White, U.K.

Illustrations by James Field (pages 4–5, 7, 9, 11, 17)
and Steve Weston (cover and pages 13, 15, 19, 21).
Diagrams by Stefan Chabluk.

Photographs: Digital Vision page12. Getty Images
pages 8, 10. istockphotos pages 6 (Andresr), 10 (Jeff
Dalton), 16 (Susan Flashman), 18 (P J Jones), 20
(Gregory Van Raalte).

Consultant: John Stidworthy, Scientific Fellow of
the Zoological Society, London, and former
Lecturer in the Education Department, Natural History
Museum, London.

Reading Adviser: Susan Kesselring, M.A., Literacy
Educator, Rosemount–Apple Valley–Eagan
(Minnesota) School District

Types of dinosaurs
In this book, a red shape at the top of a left-hand page shows the animal was a meat-eater. A green shape shows it was a plant-eater.

Just how big—or small— were they?
Dinosaurs were many different sizes. We have compared their size to one of the following:

Chicken
2 feet (60 centimeters) tall
Weight 6 pounds (2.7 kilograms)

Adult person
6 feet (1.8 meters) tall
Weight 170 pounds (76.5 kg)

Elephant
10 feet (3 m) tall
Weight 12,000 pounds
(5,400 kg)

TABLE OF CONTENTS

WHAT'S INSIDE?

Dinosaurs! These dinosaurs lived in places that now form Asia. Find out how they survived millions of years ago and what they have in common with today's animals.

LIFE IN ASIA

Dinosaurs lived between 230 million and 65 million years ago. The world did not look the same then. Much of the land and many of the seas were not in the same places as today. But even then, the land now called Asia was the biggest continent on Earth. Many kinds of dinosaurs lived all across Asia.

By the shores of a lake in what is now China, the meat-eating *Guanlong* chased plant-eating *Incisivosaurus*. Overhead glided the bird-like *Microraptor*.

MICRORAPTOR

Pronunciation:
MY-kroh-RAP-tur

Microraptor was probably the smallest dinosaur that ever lived. With feathers on its arms, legs, and tail, *Microraptor* was able to glide from tree to tree. From a distance, it must have looked like a giant butterfly.

Tree climbers today

The modern green iguana lizard can cling to tree trunks like *Microraptor* did long ago.

Size Comparison

Microraptor could cling to tree trunks like a lizard. It could also perch on branches like a bird. It was a tree-living dinosaur.

GUANLONG

Pronunciation: gwahn-LAWNG

Even though it was only the size of a stork or heron, *Guanlong* was an early relative of the big and mighty *Tyrannosaurus*. Like its large relative, *Guanlong* was a hunter, but it hunted much smaller animals. *Guanlong* had a brightly colored crest on the top of its head.

Lakeside hunter today

The black stork looks for food in shallow water, much like *Guanlong* did 160 million years ago.

Size Comparison

Guanlong hunted along the banks of streams and lakes. It found plenty of small prey to chase and eat.

INCISIVOSAURUS

Pronunciation:
in-SIZE-evo-SAW-rus

Incisivosaurus was an odd-looking dinosaur with large front teeth like a squirrel or a rabbit. This plant-eater could use its hands to grasp food. It also had long, powerful hind legs that helped it to escape from hungry meat-eating dinosaurs.

Chisel teeth today

The modern squirrel holds nuts in its paws and cracks them open with strong front teeth, much like *Incisivosaurus* did.

Size Comparison

Incisivosaurus used chisel-like front teeth to break into pine cones and nutshells to get the seeds inside. Then it used flattened teeth at the back of its mouth to grind the seeds.

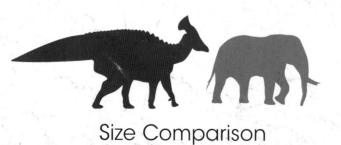

OLOROTITAN

Pronunciation:
Oh-LAW-ro-TYE-tan

Olorotitan was a big plant-eating dinosaur. It had a duck-like beak and a strange-looking crest at the back of its head. Many of the duck-billed dinosaurs had crests, which were used as signals.

Big noises today

Wolves howl through forests so that they can be heard by mates. *Olorotitan* also made a great noise to be heard by other dinosaurs.

Size Comparison

The crest of *Olorotitan* was full of air passages. The dinosaur blew air through the crest like a horn. The sound could be heard by other dinosaurs very far away.

ALIORAMUS

Pronunciation:
AL-ee-OH-rah-MUS

Alioramus was one of the biggest hunters of its time. It had long jaws, with bumpy horns along the top of its nose. Its eyes pointed forward, like those of a hunting bird, so that it could judge distances well. This helped it catch prey.

Hunting eyes today

Modern owls have eyes that point forward. This helps them to be good hunters, much like *Alioramus* once was.

Size Comparison

14

Alioramus hunted for food in forests. It used good eyesight to find animals hiding in the shadows.

PSITTACOSAURUS

Pronunciation:
si-TACK-o-SAW-rus

The name *Psittacosaurus* means "parrot lizard," and this dinosaur looked like one. It had a square head with a very large beak at the front, just like a parrot. *Psittacosaurus* used its beak to eat tough plants such as the needles of conifer trees.

Tough food today

A modern parrot uses its beak as a powerful tool to break open or crush food. *Psittacosaurus* did the same millions of years ago.

Size Comparison

Psittacosaurus walked on all fours. It used its hands to pull branches close to its mouth.

TUOJIANGOSAURUS

Pronunciation:
TOO-oh-GEE-an-GO-SAW-rus

Tuojiangosaurus was an early relative of the famous plated *Stegosaurus* of North America. The Asian dinosaur had the same spikes on the tail and smaller plates on its back. *Tuojiangosaurus* used the plates to keep away enemies, such as the big meat-eating dinosaurs of the time.

Spikes as weapons today

The hedgehog has spikes on its back that it uses to fend off hungry enemies. *Tuojiangosaurus* used its plates in the same way.

Size Comparison

Tuojiangosaurus could swing its spiked tail with great force. The dinosaur may have used its tail as a weapon to fight off enemies.

THERIZINOSAURUS

Pronunciation:
THER-i-ZEE-nuh-SAW-rus

Therizinosaurus had enormous curved claws on its hands. It used these cutting claws to rip down the branches of trees and reach the leaves that it ate. *Therizinosaurus* must have eaten plenty of leaves to feed its big body.

Big claws today

The modern sloth has large claws. It uses them to grip branches and to help collect food, like *Therizinosaurus* did.

Size Comparison

20

Therizinosaurus lived in forests. To feed, it stood on its hind legs. It could use the big claws on its front legs to hold on to branches or to rip them down.

21

Where Did They Go?

Dinosaurs are extinct, which means that none of them are alive today. Scientists study rocks and fossils to find clues about what happened to dinosaurs.

People have different explanations about what happened. Some people think a huge asteroid hit Earth and caused all sorts of climate changes, which caused the dinosaurs to die. Others think volcanic eruptions caused the climate to change and that killed the dinosaurs. No one knows for sure what happened to all of the dinosaurs.

GLOSSARY

beak—the hard front part of the mouth of birds and some dinosaurs; also known as a bill

claws—tough, usually curved fingernails or toenails

conifer—a trees that produces seeds in cones and has needle-like leaves

continent—a huge area of land like Asia and North America

crest—a structure on top of the head, usually used to signal to other animals

duck-billed—to have a broad, flat beak or bill, like that of a duck

horns—pointed structures on the head, made of bone

mates—the paired males and females of the same species, or type of animal

plate—a large, flat, usually tough structure on the body

signal—to make a sign, warning, or hint to other animals

TO LEARN MORE

AT THE LIBRARY

Clark, Neil, and William Lindsay. *1001 Facts About Dinosaurs.* New York: Backpack Books, Dorling Kindersley, 2002.

Dixon, Dougal. *Dougal Dixon's Amazing Dinosaurs.* Honesdale, Pa.: Boyds Mills Press, 2000.

Holtz, Thomas, and Michael Brett-Surman. *Dinosaur Field Guide.* New York: Random House, 2001.

ON THE WEB

FactHound offers a safe, fun way to find Web sites related to this book. All of the sites on FactHound have been researched by our staff.

1. Visit *www.facthound.com*
2. Type in this special code: 1404822615
3. Click on the FETCH IT button.

Your trusty FactHound will fetch the best Web sites for you!

INDEX

LOOK FOR ALL OF THE BOOKS IN THE DINOSAUR FIND SERIES: